# TRADING
# PLACES

## WORKBOOK FOR WOMEN

# Resources by Les and Leslie Parrott

## Books

*Becoming Soul Mates*
*The Complete Guide to Marriage Mentoring*
*Getting Ready for the Wedding*
*I Love You More* (and workbooks)
*Just the Two of Us*
*Love Is . . .*
*The Love List*
*Love Talk* (and workbooks)
*Meditations on Proverbs for Couples*
*The Parent You Want to Be*
*Pillow Talk*
*Questions Couples Ask*
*Relationships* (and workbook)
*Saving Your Marriage Before It Starts* (and workbooks)
*Saving Your Second Marriage Before It Starts* (and workbooks)
*3 Seconds*
*51 Creative Ideas for Marriage Mentors*

## Video Curriculum — ZondervanGroupware®

*Complete Resource Kit for Marriage Mentoring*
*I Love You More*
*Love Talk*
*Saving Your Marriage Before It Starts*

## Audio

*Love Talk*
*Saving Your Marriage Before It Starts*
*Saving Your Second Marriage Before It Starts*

## Books by Les Parrott

*The Control Freak*
*Helping Your Struggling Teenager*
*High Maintenance Relationships*
*The Life You Want Your Kids to Live*
*Seven Secrets of a Healthy Dating Relationship*
*Shoulda, Coulda, Woulda*
*Once Upon a Family*
*25 Ways to Win with People* (coauthored with John Maxwell)
*Love the Life You Live* (coauthored with Neil Clark Warren)

## Books by Leslie Parrott

*If You Ever Needed Friends, It's Now*
*You Matter More Than You Think*
*God Loves You Nose to Toes* (children's book)
*Marshmallow Clouds* (children's book)

THE BEST MOVE YOU'LL EVER MAKE
IN YOUR MARRIAGE

# TRADING
# PLACES

## WORKBOOK FOR WOMEN

# DRS. LES & LESLIE PARROTT

**ZONDERVAN®**

ZONDERVAN.com/
AUTHORTRACKER
*follow your favorite authors*

We want to hear from you. Please send your comments about this book to us in care of zreview@zondervan.com. Thank you.

*Trading Places Workbook for Women*
Copyright © 2008 by The Foundation for Healthy Relationships

Requests for information should be addressed to:
Zondervan, *Grand Rapids, Michigan 49530*

ISBN 978-0-310-28479-6

Published in association with Yates & Yates, LLP, Attorneys and Counselors, Suite 1000, Literary Agent, Orange, CA, and Result Source, Inc., San Diego, California.

*Interior design by Beth Shagene*

*Printed in the United States of America*

08 09 10 11 12 13 • 22 21 20 19 18 17 16 15 14 13 12 11 10 9 8 7 6 5 4 3 2 1

# Contents

# A Letter from Leslie

Someone once told me that an ideal wife is any woman who has an ideal husband. There may be some truth to that, don't you think? I mean, it's far easier to be a "good wife" when our husbands are being, doing, and saying what we like. I suppose it's the same for them too.

Regardless, I'm so glad you have chosen to use this workbook. This speaks volumes about your desire to make your marriage the best it can be. And I hope your husband is just as motivated as you are. But let me tell you, I've counseled enough women to know that husbands aren't always as gung ho as we are when it comes to doing exercises and self-tests like the ones in these workbooks. In fact, we've developed workbooks to be used with many of our other books (like *Love Talk*, *I Love You More*, and *Your Time-Starved Marriage*), and we've noticed that there are always a few more women's workbooks sold than the men's editions.

That's okay. If your husband falls into this camp, I want you to know that we've also noticed from the emails we receive that many women gain a great deal from doing the workbook exercises on their own. Of course, it's best to go through this workbook with your husband, but if he is dragging his heels at the idea, don't be too pushy. You may find that once you begin to use your workbook and talk about it with him, his curiosity will be piqued and he'll join you.

## Why a Workbook?

We've always enjoyed this quote from comedian Woody Allen: "I took a speed-reading course and read *War and Peace* in twenty minutes. It involves Russia."

Ever felt like that after reading a book? Sometimes it becomes so easy to focus on finishing a book that we miss its main message. What you hold in your hands is an insurance policy against that happening while you are reading *Trading Places*. But it's also more than that.

Books let us shake hands with new ideas, but these ideas remain as flat as the printed page if we do not apply them to our lives. For this reason, we have designed a workbook that will help you incorporate into your relationship the new lessons you learn while reading. And we've designed it to be used either individually or in a small group setting.

## For Individual and Couple Study

As you read through the main book, you will discover a place at the end of each chapter where it points you to do an exercise in this workbook. Most of the exercises are designed to take about five or ten minutes. You and your husband will usually work on them separately, then compare your results — that's why it's important to each have your own individual workbook. Or, you may sometimes work on an exercise together so that you can put a new principle into practice. This is where real learning occurs and where new ideas become more than acquaintances; they begin to make a positive difference in your marriage.

We have used these exercises with countless couples, both in our counseling practice as well as in our seminar settings. They are proven and they work. And that's why we are passionate about you doing them as you read through our book. You just may find that the time you invest in doing these exercises with your husband pays some of the greatest dividends you could hope for.

While there is no one right way to use these workbooks, we suggest that you complete the exercises as you encounter them in the book, or soon after you have finished reading the chapter that covers the exercise. The point is to integrate the exercises into the process of reading the book.

We hope you'll make the material your own as you proceed through these pages. Don't get too hung up on following the rules. If a particular exercise leads you down a more intriguing path, take it. Some of these exercises may simply serve as springboards to discussions that better fit your style. However, if an exercise seems challenging, don't give up on it. As the saying goes, anything worth having is worth working for — especially when it comes to your marriage.

So, whether you are a speed-reader or not, we hope you don't approach the *Trading Places Workbook* as just another item to check off on your "to-do" list. We hope and pray that you will instead use these exercises, self-tests, and discussion questions to internalize the book's message and fortify your relationship by trading places.

Leslie Parrott
Seattle, Washington

# EXERCISE
## ONE

# Exploring Your Own
# Social Style

Accurately identifying your social style is essential to trading places. We've developed an online assessment, the Trading Places Inventory, for helping you do just that. The exercise here centers on this assessment. We're providing you with a paper-pencil version of the assessment in this workbook just in case you don't have access to a computer. This will require you to tabulate your scores yourself, and it won't provide the instant graphic depiction of your social style, but it still does the job.

If you have already taken the assessment, skip to the bottom of this exercise for some additional suggestions.

## The Trading Places Inventory

Below are a number of pairs of personal characteristics or traits. For each pair, choose the trait that describes you more than it describes your partner. Mark A if you are more "imaginative," or B if you value being "rational" when compared to your partner. Some of the traits will appear twice, but always in combination with a different trait. There are no right or wrong answers. Please be honest.

# I Am More ...

1.  a  imaginative          b  rational
2.  a  helpful              b  quick-witted
3.  a  neat                 b  sympathetic
4.  a  level-headed         b  efficient
5.  a  intelligent          b  considerate
6.  a  self-reliant         b  ambitious
7.  a  respectful           b  original
8.  a  creative             b  sensible
9.  a  generous             b  individualistic
10. a  responsible          b  original
11. a  capable              b  tolerant
12. a  trustworthy          b  wise
13. a  neat                 b  logical
14. a  forgiving            b  gentle
15. a  efficient            b  respectful
16. a  alert                b  cooperative
17. a  imaginative          b  helpful
18. a  realistic            b  moral
19. a  considerate          b  wise
20. a  sympathetic          b  individualistic
21. a  ambitious            b  patient

Now take a moment to score the first part of this questionnaire. Give yourself a point for each answer that matches the following key. Note that items 1, 4, 6, 8, 10, and 13 are "buffer" items and are not used in the scoring.

| | | |
|---|---|---|
| 2.  a  ____ | 11.  b  ____ | 17.  a  ____ |
| 3.  b  ____ | 12.  a  ____ | 18.  b  ____ |
| 5.  b  ____ | 14.  a  ____ | 19.  a  ____ |
| 7.  a  ____ | 15.  b  ____ | 20.  a  ____ |
| 9.  a  ____ | 16.  b  ____ | 21.  b  ____ |

TOTAL: _____

Now answer the following questions by circling a number beside each of the items below.

|  | Rarely or none of the time | A little of the time | Some of the time | A good part of the time | Most or all of the time |
|---|---|---|---|---|---|
| 1. When my partner and I have a disagreement, I win. | 1 | 2 | 3 | 4 | 5 |
| 2. I'm more hard-driving than my partner. | 1 | 2 | 3 | 4 | 5 |
| 3. I'm very good at solving problems for my partner. | 1 | 2 | 3 | 4 | 5 |
| 4. Compared to my partner, I keep my feelings in check. | 1 | 2 | 3 | 4 | 5 |
| 5. I'm good at accurately analyzing a situation or issue in our marriage. | 1 | 2 | 3 | 4 | 5 |

15

| | Rarely or none of the time | A little of the time | Some of the time | A good part of the time | Most or all of the time |
|---|---|---|---|---|---|
| 6. I'm a natural problem solver. | 1 | 2 | 3 | 4 | 5 |
| 7. Compared to my partner, I confront conflict head-on. | 1 | 2 | 3 | 4 | 5 |
| 8. I'm assertive. | 1 | 2 | 3 | 4 | 5 |
| 9. Relative to my partner, I'm more goal-oriented. | 1 | 2 | 3 | 4 | 5 |
| 10. I like to get to the facts more than my partner. | 1 | 2 | 3 | 4 | 5 |
| 11. I have more "rules" about doing things than my partner. | 1 | 2 | 3 | 4 | 5 |
| 12. I feel my partner is emotional. | 1 | 2 | 3 | 4 | 5 |
| 13. I take control more than my partner does. | 1 | 2 | 3 | 4 | 5 |
| 14. Compared to my partner, I would rather zero in on a solution than explore feelings. | 1 | 2 | 3 | 4 | 5 |
| 15. I'm less sentimental than my partner. | 1 | 2 | 3 | 4 | 5 |
| 16. I'm not easy to please because my expectations are high. | 1 | 2 | 3 | 4 | 5 |
| 17. Compared to my partner, I'm more likely to criticize and pressure people to get things done. | 1 | 2 | 3 | 4 | 5 |

_Rarely or none of the time_
_A little of the time_
_Some of the time_
_A good part of the time_
_Most or all of the time_

18. I have no problem making
    my own needs known.                    1  2  3  4  5

19. Compared to my partner,
    I'm less likely to show my emotions.    1  2  3  4  5

20. I want to be in control more
    than my partner does.                  1  2  3  4  5

Score this self-test by totaling up your points on the items.
There is a potential score of 20 to 100.

TOTAL: _____

The two parts of this questionnaire give you two sub-scores.
The first half of the test reveals your "Heart Score" while
the second half reveals your "Head Score." You can note
them here:

YOUR HEART SCORE: _____

YOUR HEAD SCORE: _____

# Making Sense of Your
# *Trading Places* Self-Test

There are 15 possible points on the first section of this self-test (your Heart Score). If you scored 7 points or more, you are probably in the "high heart" zone. Below 7 points puts you in the "low heart" zone. Note your heart score on this continuum.

Low Heart Score                              High Heart Score

1                        7                        15

There are 100 points on the Head Talk Test (indicating where you are in your inclination to analyze). If you scored 50 or higher on this test, you are probably in the "high head" zone. Note your head score on this continuum.

Low Head Score                             High Head Score

20                        70                    100

Are both of your scores high? Congratulations! You've learned to balance your head and your heart. This creates an optimal balance for trading places. You've probably worked at this and are adept at using both when trying to make a meaningful connection with your spouse. You sympathize as well as analyze. In other words, you empathize. You possess the precious secret to effectively trade places.

Now perhaps you scored low on both your head and heart components; you neither sympathize nor analyze. That's okay. This simply means you presently tend to personalize more than empathize. In other words, for a number of possible reasons, you currently have a tough time seeing beyond your own boundaries. Chances are you're carrying some emotional pain. Perhaps you've been burned in a previous relationship, and like the turtle retreating into its shell, you currently withdraw in order to feel safe, to not get burned again. It's only natural, and you shouldn't feel guilty for being in this place. With time and effort, as well as patience from your partner, you'll move beyond it.

Now let's get something clear before we go any further: if you or your partner's scores don't happen to land you in the territory of empathy — if you or your partner tend to sympathize but not analyze or vice versa, or if you or your partner tend to do neither — don't feel bad, not even for a minute. You're not alone. The vast majority of couples are in the same boat. That's why we wrote *Trading Places*. Every couple, no matter their age or stage, can learn to move into mutual empathy with a few pointers and some intentional effort.

For now, simply identify which category of social style you tend to fall into. Based on your scores, which of these four categories is the one where you rest most often?

- ☐ **The Sympathizer:** More Feeling than Thinking
- ☐ **The Personalizer:** Short on Both Feeling and Thinking
- ☐ **The Analyzer:** More Thinking than Feeling
- ☐ **The Empathizer:** A Good Measure of Both Thinking and Feeling

After taking this assessment, make an educated guess about where you fall into the Trading Places Matrix. Draw a square within the following diagram to represent where you fall on the head and heart continuums.

## The Four Social Styles

**FEELING**
Emotional Intuiting

|  | HIGH | LOW |
| --- | --- | --- |
| LOW | Sympathizer | Personalizer |
| HIGH | Empathizer | Analyzer |

**THINKING**
Cognitive Understanding

Compare notes with your husband. Which category does he tend to fall into most frequently? What do your two styles say about the road ahead for you two in learning to trade places?

_____

_____

_____

_____

# EXERCISE
## TWO

# Getting What
# You Want

The bottom line of trading places is to ensure that you are getting what you want from your marriage — and that your husband is too. What most couples never figure out is that trading places is the best way of doing just that.

The exercise on the next page is designed to help you articulate what it is that you want most. If you've read the chapter in the book on this topic, you know that we identified eight items that trading places is sure to help you achieve. From that list, what do you value most and what do you value least? Place a 1 next to the desire that's most important to you, and number on down the list to 8 for the item on this list that is least important to you.

# If I Could Press
# a Magic Button for My Marriage,
# I'd Most Like ...

\_\_\_\_ A reduction in critical comments

\_\_\_\_ The elimination of nagging

\_\_\_\_ A sure way to short-circuit conflict

\_\_\_\_ A means to becoming better friends

\_\_\_\_ The tools for developing a deeper commitment

\_\_\_\_ A sure way to give and get grace from each other

\_\_\_\_ The benefit of living longer and healthier lives

\_\_\_\_ A boost in realizing our dreams together

Why did you rank your number one item highest on your list?

_____

_____

What else is on your wish list? If you had three more wishes that could come true about changes you'd like to see happen in your relationship (how you interact with each other), what would they be? Even if they are small, note them here:

_____

_____

_____

Once your husband has completed this same exercise, compare notes. What ranks highest for him? What did he note as his three additional wishes? Discuss why you each chose what you did and what your marriage would look and feel like if both of these desires were realized.

Also discuss how you would know that these wishes had been fulfilled. In other words, once you finish this study on *Trading Places*, how will you know if your personal goals are being reached? In fact, write down what your marriage would look like if you were getting what you want. Be objective. Paint a picture of married life with this desire fulfilled.

---

Now rank your level of optimism about getting your desires fulfilled. How optimistic are you that you will find improvement by going through this program on *Trading Places?*

Pessimistic                                             Optimistic

| 1 | 2 | 3 | 4 | 5 | 6 | 7 | 8 | 9 | 10 |

Why did you rank your level as you did?

What do you see, personally, as your biggest hurdle to getting what you'd like?

_____

_____

_____

What can you do, personally, to increase your chances of getting what you want?

_____

_____

_____

※

This exercise will serve as a way to measure your progress as you go through the remaining chapters of the book. In fact, you may want to revisit this exercise as you move along. Keeping your goal in mind as you make your journey is one of the best things you can do to ensure that you reach your goal.

Again, discuss your answers with your spouse and do your best to put yourself in his shoes as he talks to you about why he answered as he did. He'll be doing the same for you.

# EXERCISE
# THREE

# Knowing What You Feel

"Knowing thyself," says Steven Pinker, "is a way of making thyself as palatable as possible to others." We agree, especially when it comes to knowing our own emotions. As you already know, emotional clarity enables you to manage your moods and become much better at trading places. This exercise will help you do just that.

On the following scale, rate how adept you are (in your own opinion) at knowing what you feel and being able to articulate your emotions at any given moment:

Poor                                                              Excellent

| 1 | 2 | 3 | 4 | 5 | 6 | 7 | 8 | 9 | 10 |

Now, explain why you rated yourself as you did (be specific):

_____

_____

What are your emotional "triggers"? In other words, what do you notice going on in your body when you feel an emotion like anger or excitement? Many researchers consider physiological arousal — in the form of increased heart rate, change in breathing, face becoming hot, or hands becoming cold, for example — the defining feature of emotion. So what are some of the specific physiological clues that let you know you're experiencing the following emotions?

Anger: _____

_____

Sadness: _____

_____

Joy: _____

_____

Disgust: _____

_____

Surprise: _____

_____

Fear: _____

_____

By the way, these are considered the six primary emotions. They involve unique and consistent behavioral displays across cultures.

How did your family of origin shape your emotional experiences? On the following scale, rate the expression of emotions in the home you grew up in:

Very Unexpressive                                    Very Expressive

| 1 | 2 | 3 | 4 | 5 | 6 | 7 | 8 | 9 | 10 |

On the same scale, write your spouse's name under the number you think best describes the level of emotional expressiveness of his home when he was growing up.

Provide a brief example that typifies emotional expressiveness in your home as a child:

_____

_____

Finally, on the following scale, rate how adept you are (in your own opinion) at managing your own emotions (controlling and communicating them):

Managed Poorly                                  Managed Very Well

| 1 | 2 | 3 | 4 | 5 | 6 | 7 | 8 | 9 | 10 |

Again, explain why you rated yourself as you did (be specific):

_____

_____

Do you think that as a woman, your emotional experiences differ significantly from your husband? Assuming you think so, explain how:

_____

_____

If your husband is like most men, he is more likely than you to express emotions that don't feel supportive of your relationship. In other words, he is more apt to express anger. Why? Because men, in comparison to women, generally are prone to express more anger in marriage. And anger, from a woman's perspective, can feel more threatening to a marriage than it does for a man. So how can this improve your ability to empathize with your husband? Would it be helpful to recognize that anger probably doesn't make him as uncomfortable as it does you? Why or why not?

_____

_____

_____

## Comparing Notes

Once you have both independently completed this exercise in your respective workbooks, take a few minutes to compare your responses and to answer the following questions. And as always, remember to remain nonjudgmental as you explore this sometimes sensitive issue.

1. Discuss how each of you rated your own abilities to articulate your emotions. Do you agree with each other's self-ratings? Why or why not?

_____

_____

_____

2.  How do the levels of emotional expressiveness in your childhood homes compare to one another? How does this impact the home you've created together? What do each of you find healthy and positive about one another's childhood homes in this area?

   _____

   _____

   _____

3.  Compare your answers on how you each manage your own emotions. If you're feeling particularly brave, invite your husband to give you feedback on how you are doing in this area and how you might improve.

   _____

   _____

   _____

4.  Discuss your gender differences as they relate to your emotions. What can you learn from each other as the opposite sex? And what can you do to better understand one another's emotional experiences?

   _____

   _____

   _____

5. Talk about your joint opinions concerning the main point of this exercise: Empathy builds on self-aware-ness—and the more open we are to our own emotions, the more skilled we become in reading our spouse's. How much do you agree or disagree and why?

_____

_____

_____

## Taking It Deeper

If you are especially motivated to "know what you feel," we want you to be aware of what numerous research studies have found. It's actually quite simple. If you want to enjoy more emotional clarity, keep track of your emotions for five days. How? By writing in a journal. Every couple of hours or so, simply reflect on how you have been feeling since your last journal entry. If you do this for five days, you will be positively amazed at how self-aware you become.

# EXERCISE
## FOUR

# Checking Your Ego
# at the Door

If you are to ever effectively trade places with your partner, it will be because you take the first critical step to temporarily set aside your own agenda. And to do that you will need to keep your ego in check, which is no small feat for many of us. But remember, this does *not* mean you will sacrifice your own needs — it simply means you'll briefly set them in abeyance while you begin trading places.

Let's begin with a little self-test that will require you to be brutally honest with yourself. In the table below, place a mark in the column nearest to the statement that best matches how you feel. If you strongly agree with the statement on the right, mark the 5 box, putting a 5 in it. If you don't know, mark the 3, putting a 3 in it. If you strongly agree with the statement on the left, mark the 1 box, putting a 1 in it.

Again, be honest with yourself as your choose between the sets of statements.

| Left | 1 | 2 | 3 | 4 | 5 | Right |
|------|---|---|---|---|---|-------|
| I often doubt my view of things. | | | | | | My view of things is always correct. |
| I don't mind being wrong. | | | | | | I hate to be wrong. |
| I look for valid criticisms so I can improve. | | | | | | Criticisms of me are not true. |
| I know I can usually correct my mistakes. | | | | | | It is very important to never make a mistake. |
| If you contradict me, I look to see if you are correct. | | | | | | If you contradict me, you are obviously wrong. |
| If you make a good argument, I can easily change my view. | | | | | | I automatically defend my viewpoint, no matter what the other person says. |
| It doesn't bother me to lose an argument. | | | | | | If I lose an argument, I feel bad inside. |
| I look for the value in other people's arguments. | | | | | | Other people's arguments are worthless. |
| The real truth is more important than my view. | | | | | | My view is the real truth. |
| Subtotal scores (add across this row) | | | | | | =      (total score) |

**Scoring:** Add up all the numbers in the five columns. Then add the subtotals in the last row (across the five columns) to achieve your total score. It should fall within the range of 9 to 45.

Write your total score here: _____

If your answers are accurate, here's what your score means:

**9 to 19** — Your score indicates that you have relatively few egocentric tendencies in your disposition. In other words, relative to other people, you are less inclined to be focused on yourself. This bodes very well for your capacity to set aside your own agenda as you attempt to trade places with your spouse. You already tend to do this quite instinctively. If your score is on the especially low end of this range, however, you may need to give special attention to making sure you express your own needs more forthrightly. You may need to exert more assertiveness and so on. You can do this by simply finishing this sentence more often: "If it were up to me, I would ..." This allows you to be more upfront with your own needs while still maintaining a healthy other-focused perspective.

**20 to 35** — Your score is in the midrange of egocentric tendencies. This means you are inclined to sometimes set your own needs aside brilliantly, but at other times you will struggle to do so. In fact, these difficult times may be quite predictable. For many people who score in this range, the selfish tendencies appear most when they are feeling hungry, stressed, or tired. Is this the case for you? If so, the simple acknowledgment of this fact can sometimes be enough to help you remedy the situation. You can say something like, "I'm having a tough time focusing on anyone other than myself at the moment because ..." This will help you and your spouse recognize that it's not the most opportune time for you to set your own needs aside.

**36 to 45** — Your score indicates an intense level of ego-centric tendencies. This means you have a tough time set-ting aside your own agenda because of a fear that your own needs may not get met. Because of this, you will need to give special attention to setting your own needs on the back burner. At times this may be a very deep struggle for you, but with a little practice you can make significant improve-ments. Begin by acknowledging that this is true. You may not want to face this fact, but once you do, you will have taken a big step in changing this self-centered focus. Second, realize that this is only temporary. To trade places you're not required to go forever without getting your own needs met. In fact, just the opposite is true. Once you enjoy mutual empathy, your needs will get met like never before.

Next, complete this sentence when you are ready to set your own needs aside: "If I were my spouse, I would feel or think ..." You can also complete this sentence to your-self: "My spouse has a valid point because ..." Both of these sentence stems will get you out of your egocentric focus and allow you to take this first step toward trading places. They're a way of doing a simple self-exercise: If you were in an irritable mood and projecting negative energy towards your spouse, visualize for a moment that your spouse is you. Do you appreciate the way you are being treated? That's the key question for you, and it will help you transcend your own ego.

Once you have reviewed the meaning of your personal score on this self-test, compare with your spouse and talk about where the two of you tend to line up on the following continuum. Place your name and his name at the appropriate places:

| 9 | 25 | 45 |
|---|---|---|

- How do your scores compare? Do you both agree with where you landed? Why or why not?

  _____

  _____

  _____

- Which one of you may have the tougher time setting aside your own agenda? How can you help each other do this better?

  _____

  _____

  _____

- Are there predictable times when you think your self-centered ways are most likely to interfere with your attempts to trade places? What are they?

  _____

  _____

  _____

## The Switching Method
## to Setting Aside Your Own Agenda

Before we leave the exercise for this chapter, we want to give you a practical tool for taking this first step on a specific issue that may be difficult for both of you to see from the same perspective. Do you have an issue like that in mind? To use this method you will need something specific in mind. Here's what to do:

First, on a sheet of paper, write out all of your beliefs about why your perspective is right (this is the easy part!).

Next, switch sides. Put your own beliefs aside for a moment and write down all the reasons you can think of that indicate your spouse's perspective (his beliefs and feelings) is right and you are wrong.

Now, reflect on both sides and consider the truth in both perspectives. Discuss any new insights you have gained.

# EXERCISE
## FIVE

# Reading Your Partner
# Like a Book

The key to effectively reading your spouse is to be completely objective—having an empty cup so to speak. Overcoming your biases, prejudices, and projections related to your husband is essential. Objectivity is impossible without doing this. So let's start with a straightforward self-assessment. Which statement best indicates how you see your own objectivity level when it comes to interacting with your husband?

☐ I'm almost always objective when interacting
with my husband.

☐ I'm better than average at being objective
with my husband.

☐ I'm somewhat objective when interacting
with my husband.

☐ I'm less than average at being objective
with my husband.

☐ I'm rarely objective when interacting
with my husband.

Why did you rate yourself the way you did? In other words, if you had to justify to a stranger that your self-assessment on objectivity is accurate, what evidence would you point to?

_____

_____

### Free Your Husband
### from "Always" and "Never"

One of the most common ways we lose our objectivity with our spouse is to begin a sentence with either of the following two stems. Complete each of them in relationship to your husband with the first negative sentiment that comes into your mind:

You always ... _____

_____

You never ... _____

_____

Of course, whenever we make these statements, we realize deep down that they are not really true. Your husband is not "always" late or emotional, or whatever. But in saying he is, you put him in a box and lose your objectivity. Would it make any difference if you changed the sentences you wrote by saying, "You sometimes ..."? The research says it would. So why don't you rewrite each of these sentences with more objectivity in mind:

You sometimes . . . _____

_____

You sometimes . . . _____

_____

Do you see how this can alter your attitude and make you more accurate in reading your husband? It really does help.

## Ask Open-Ended Questions

If you are sincerely motivated to read your husband like a book, you've got to master the art of the open-ended question—the kind that cannot be answered with a simple "yes" or "no." Here are some examples:

- "Could you tell me more about that?"
- "Can you help me understand that a little better?"
- "How was that for you?"

Now, compare these questions to something like: "Are you sure about that?" That's a closed-ended question because it doesn't generate a free-flow in the conversation and it does nothing to help you read your husband.

You get the idea. But putting these open-ended questions into practice can be challenging—especially if you lose your objectivity and are overcome with emotional intensity. So, right now, while you are calm and cool, consider a topic that often gets heated between you and your husband. It could be about money, in-laws, the kids, or anything else. Think about his statements on this issue and write down a couple specific open-ended questions you can pose to him the next time you're covering this topic:

_____

_____

## Step Outside the Box

In your own opinion, what is most likely to keep you from accurately reading your spouse's moods, motives, attitudes, and actions?

I tend to put him in an emotional box by saying things like, "You always get so angry when we talk about ..." or "You never want to hear my point of view when we talk about ..."

Never                                                    Frequently

1    2    3    4    5    6    7    8    9    10

I psychologize him by saying things like, "You've got issues that you need to work on" or "You're so reactive on this topic."

Never                                                    Frequently

1    2    3    4    5    6    7    8    9    10

I tend to label his feelings by saying things like, "You're obviously angry . . . or jealous . . . or . . ."

Never                                              Frequently

| 1 | 2 | 3 | 4 | 5 | 6 | 7 | 8 | 9 | 10 |
|---|---|---|---|---|---|---|---|---|----|

❊

The three items above are simply to get your wheels turning. In what specific way are you most likely to lose your objectivity with your husband by putting him in a box? It may be that you tend to project a specific emotion, attitude, or behavior on him, and because of this you rarely see outside of this box. What is it?

_____

_____

_____


## Avoid the "High-Risk" Responses

Communication experts have identified several categories of responses that almost always make a person clam up when we say them. When we use them we risk interfering with the potential to accurately understand our spouse. Why? Because they take the focus off of our husband. These responses are almost certain to cause him to quit sharing from the heart. On the next page is a list of the most common high-risk responses (along with an example).

Order the top three categories of high-risk responses that you are most likely to use in conversations with your husband.

_____ **Ordering**—"You can't do that."

_____ **Threatening**—"I'm warning you right now."

_____ **Moralizing**—"You should really know better."

_____ **Advising**—"I can tell you what's best for you."

_____ **Questioning**—"Did you even think about asking me first?"

_____ **Judging**—"You are way out of line."

_____ **Condescending**—"You're a regular genius."

_____ **Diagnosing**—"You're being paranoid."

_____ **Reassuring**—"There's no need to worry about this."

_____ **Diverting**—"Think about the positive side."

## Use the Onion Theory

When it comes to turning on your emotional radar, it can help to think of your husband as an onion. Sounds strange, we know, but stay with us.

The outermost layer is your husband's most superficial aspect of who he really is. It's the side of him that a stranger sitting next to him on a bus would see. But as you peel back that outermost layer, you'll find additional layers that get to his attitudes, and deeper layers that reveal his goals and personal problems. And still deeper layers contain his darkest thoughts and fears that he probably doesn't even want to acknowledge to himself.

The extent to which you can "read" him is determined by how many of his layers you're able to get him to reveal. And here's a little secret: Your husband will generally reveal his layers in direct proportion to you revealing yours. This is the onion theory in a nutshell. If you maintain your self-disclosure at a surface level, he's likely to do the same. Vulnerability tends to beget vulnerability. That's not always easy for a wife to do, but once you put the onion theory into practice, you'll be a believer.

## Talking It Over

Now that you have completed each of the little sections of this exercise, take some time together to compare notes and talk through your answers. Cover each section and gently explore where the two of you are coming from. The goal is to help you better "read" each other.

Finally, write down the one specific thing you will do differently as a result of this exercise:

_____

_____

# EXERCISE
## SIX

# Improving Your Care IQ

So how do you measure up when it comes to cultivating a positive care quotient with your husband? Do you make him feel loved . . .

- On occasion?
- Much of the time?
- All the time?

Take this quiz and find out. Check the box next to the answer that most accurately represents your view of your care quotient. Be as honest as you can. We'll have some practical helps and suggestions for you at the end of this exercise.

1. The word that most aptly describes you is:

☐ Compassionate

☐ Kind

☐ Generous

2. If your husband brings home news of a major disappointment from his workplace, you are likely to say:

☐ "I know how I'd feel if that happened to me, but how are you feeling?"

☐ "I'm so sorry, but you have so many other good things going for you."

☐ "You must feel devastated; I can't imagine how hurt you feel."

3. When I'm choosing a birthday gift for my husband, I ...

☐ Try to make it as personal and meaningful as possible.

☐ Try to make it as fun and exciting as possible.

☐ Try to make it as useful and economical as possible.

4. Which of the three statements below do you believe is the most accurate?

☐ Doing loving things is more important than *being* loving.

☐ Being loving is more important than *doing* loving things.

☐ Either you're loving or you aren't.

5. When I'm having a disagreement with my husband, I ...

    ☐ Try to understand his position before trying to get him to understand mine.

    ☐ Try to resolve it by giving in to his side even if I know I'm right.

    ☐ Try to get my perspective heard clearly, regardless of the outcome.

6. One of my biggest hurdles to being a loving person is ...

    ☐ Self-focus

    ☐ A judgmental attitude

    ☐ Apathy

7. Which statement do you hear most often from your husband?

    ☐ "You always know just how I feel and just what to say."

    ☐ "You're sometimes so eager to meet my needs, you meet needs I don't have."

    ☐ "I know you love me, but sometimes I have to remind myself."

8. Everyone walks the first mile in a relationship—just to be a decent person. How often do you walk the extra mile for your husband?

   ☐ Often

   ☐ Sometimes

   ☐ Rarely

9. Do you agree that the heart of a loving relationship is putting yourself in the other person's shoes?

   ☐ Yes—even if it means you might get a few blisters now and then.

   ☐ Most of the time—but that doesn't mean I give up my own shoes.

   ☐ Only when the person's shoes are the same size as mine.

10. One of the things I'm likely to do to let my husband know I love him is . . .

   ☐ Treat him with a special backrub or something else he enjoys.

   ☐ Let him go out with his guy friends without making him feel guilty.

   ☐ Cook a favorite meal or take him to his favorite restaurant.

11. If he needs me to pick up his prescription at the drug-store, even when I'm especially busy, I typically …

☐ Run the errand without much complaining.

☐ Try to do it, but let him know how difficult it will be.

☐ Tell him it simply will not work with my schedule.

**Answer Key:**

Circle your responses. Then add up the number of ●'s, ■'s, and ◆'s you have, per the chart below. Write the numbers in the spaces provided.

|   | 1 | 2 | 3 | 4 | 5 | 6 | 7 | 8 | 9 | 10 | 11 |
|---|---|---|---|---|---|---|---|---|---|----|----|
| a | ● | ● | ● | ■ | ● | ● | ● | ● | ● | ● | ● |
| b | ■ | ◆ | ■ | ● | ■ | ■ | ■ | ■ | ■ | ◆ | ■ |
| c | ◆ | ■ | ◆ | ◆ | ◆ | ◆ | ◆ | ◆ | ◆ | ◆ | ■ | ◆ |

● _____

■ _____

◆ _____

# What Your Answers Mean

## Mostly ●'s

Assuming you answered honestly, you not only *do* loving things, you *are* a loving person and your husband knows it. Nobody mistakes you for a phony wannabe. You're the real deal—a genuinely caring spouse with a genius-level care quotient. You know how to make your husband feel understood and cared for. Because of this, he is far more likely to open up to you than the average spouse. You have developed a special gift that will bring many blessings to your marriage. Of course, all this is contingent on how honestly you answered these items and whether your husband concurs. So take some time to review your answers with him to get a "reality check." If he's in agreement, you're to be congratulated! But we still have some recommendations for you:

### What To Do

☑ Do something just for you. When was the last time you enjoyed a leisurely latte while reading a good book? Or how about taking a long bubble bath in the middle of the day? Because you are so good at meeting other people's needs, you may never indulge yourself.

☑ Allow others to serve you. Your spouse surprises you with breakfast in bed. How do you feel? Does a twinge of guilt run through your body? Relax. You need to receive the love of others as well as you give your love to them.

☑ Keep doing what you're doing. Your friends are drawn to you because they like the way you make them feel. Wherever you are is the safest place on earth for your family members. Protect your loving ways by recharging your batteries and relishing the gift you are to those around you.

## Mostly ■'s

You are a loving person who works hard to make your husband feel loved — even when you don't feel like it. The problem you run into sometimes is that you do the right thing for the wrong reasons. You may give him a birthday gift, for example, only to have it checked off your to-do list, not to really celebrate his birthday. And sometimes he knows it. On the whole, your care quotient is strong and your concern for him is evident, but in your struggle to be the loving person you want to be, you can benefit from a few pointers:

### What To Do

☑ Focus on your most loving qualities. Maybe you're an especially good listener. Perhaps you know how to choose the perfect gift. Or maybe you have a knack for noticing when someone is feeling lonely. This loving ability you have will become your trademark. Don't neglect it.

☑ Celebrate others' successes. Most people find it easy to care for a friend who just lost a job or received some disappointing news. But a truly loving person also celebrates a friend's accomplishments. The same holds true for your spouse. Take notice when he does something well. Recognize it. Celebrate it. It may be one of the most loving things you ever do for him.

☑ Keep your motivation in check. The next time you do something loving for your husband, ask yourself why you're doing it. If it's out of guilt, for example, you'll need to realign your motivation. After all, everyone has a built-in radar detector for insincere motivations — including your husband. And nobody likes a guilt gift.

## Mostly ◆'s

You want to be a loving person, but you sometimes struggle to do the loving things you know you want to do for your husband. There are a myriad of stumbling blocks on your path from good intentions to good, caring actions. From time to time, you may be tired, cranky, self-absorbed, or even oblivious. Whatever the reason, you are going to need to ramp up your efforts to cultivate a stronger care quotient and make him feel loved. In addition to making sure you're practicing the first two steps to trading places (covered in chapters 4 and 5 in the book), here are a few more suggestions.

## What To Do

☑ Generate gratitude. The more thankful you are, the more loving you become. Make a list of things you appreciate about your husband and your marriage. When you are with him, try to recall what you have on that list and let him know what you appreciate. Say it out loud.

☑ Center yourself. To increase your care quotient, you've got to be fully present in your conversations with your husband, not distracted (e.g., talking on your cell phone or watching television). You need to make him feel like he is the only person on the planet when you are with him. The more at peace you are with yourself, the better you will be at this important quality. So the next time you're in a conversation, relax. Set aside your to-do list and focus on his feelings and what he is saying.

☑ Review chapter 3 of *Trading Places*, "The Prerequisite for Trading Places." This will help you survey your own emotional terrain. And while this may seem self-serving on the surface, it's actually essential to being able to understand your husband's feelings and to convey your care for him.

## Do at Least One Thing Today to Improve Your Care IQ

Take a few minutes to reflect practically on your life and your husband. As you "walk through your day," in what ways can you show more care for him? If you were in his shoes at various points in the day, what would you enjoy hearing or receiving or knowing about you?

Make a quick list of whatever comes to mind. It could be anything from helping him do a household project, leaving him a quick and caring message on his phone, or giving him a "night of passion," and so on.

Once you've made your list, put yourself in his shoes by (1) setting aside your own agenda, (2) turning on your emotional radar, and (3) asking yourself, What one thing could I do today, to improve my care quotient for my husband?

Now carry it out.

# EXERCISE
## SEVEN

# Maximizing the eHarmony
# Marriage Program

Whether you choose to participate in the online eHarmony program or not, this exercise will help you tune into each other in an effort to more accurately understand what you'd like to achieve in your marriage right now. And if you do end up availing yourselves of the online program, completing this exercise will certainly cultivate an even more positive experience.

Simply answer the following questions as honestly as you can. Once you have completed the questions, share your answers with your spouse.

If you could press a magic button right now to make you a better wife, what one specific thing would you improve?

_____

_____

_____

Name one specific desire you would like to have fulfilled more frequently in your marriage. In other words, what one single relationship improvement would make you a happier wife?

_____

_____

_____

_____

_____

If you were married to yourself, what would you find to be most challenging and why?

_____

_____

_____

_____

If you were married to yourself, what would you find to be most rewarding and why?

_____

_____

_____

_____

On the following scale, how inclined are you to delve into the online eHarmony Marriage program:

Not inclined                                    Inclined

| 1 | 2 | 3 | 4 | 5 | 6 | 7 | 8 | 9 | 10 |

Why did you answer as you did? Explain your inclination:

_____

_____

_____

_____

_____

_____

_____

# EXERCISE
## EIGHT

# Getting Your Partner
# to See through Your Eyes

As promised, this exercise will help you put the chapter's six suggestions to work for you. Here you'll find some specific guidance in three targeted areas that are personalized to you. Each has been proven to work for countless couples.

## Sharing Your "Highs" and "Lows"

This little tip can help you carve a healthy groove into your marriage that will work wonders for getting your spouse to see your side. It's a quick and simple journey through the highs and lows of your day. For example, in the space below, write down the thing that gave you the greatest satisfaction or joy in the past twenty-four hours:

_____

_____

Now write down the thing that caused you the greatest consternation or uneasiness:

_____

_____

That's it. Well, almost. Now you need to invite your husband to do the same. After all, you're both helping each other to see the other side together. And if you have more than just a couple minutes on your hands to do this, you can both reveal two "highs" and two "lows" from your day. You get the idea. By doing this daily, your husband will be far more tuned into you, and thus, far more likely to trade places.

## Set Out the Right Pair of Shoes

Okay. Are you ready for the easiest way you'll ever find to get your husband to empathize with you? Drumroll ... tell him how you're feeling. Well, that's obvious! Right? Don't be so quick to pass judgment on this tip. Far too many wives want their husbands to know what they need without having to say it out loud. You want him to know instinctively what you're thinking or feeling. But, of course, he can't read your mind. You have to tell him. It doesn't matter how adept he is at empathy, he needs help from you to know which of your shoes he should step into.

The best way to do this is by completing the "I need you ..." sentence stem. Here are some examples:

### I need you to ...

- give me more space.
- help me accomplish this task.
- compliment me on this project.
- help the kids quiet down.
- show me more respect by ...

What do you need most right now, this very moment in time, from your husband? Be specific and write it down:

_____

_____

Like the "high/low" tip, you can do this daily. Both of you. You can set a time (like when you are both home at the end of your day), or you can make it more spontaneous by saying, "You now what I need most from you right now?" This eases the pressure of having to read each other's minds.

## Highlight Your Most Important Emotional Needs

Okay. So this one gets a bit more personal and will require some reflection, but it can go a very long way in helping your spouse enter your world on a more consistent basis. The key is to help him see with as much clarity as possible your deepest emotional needs. Don't worry. This doesn't require Dr. Freud. Here's the most proven method for getting at this quickly.

In the space below, note the needs you had as a child that seldom got met by your mom or dad. You'll probably have a different need in each case. Record this by placing a check mark in the appropriate column. Of course, you will have some items with no check marks since they were not an unmet emotional need or because they weren't important to you. Only note those needs that you longed to have fulfilled but that you felt rarely were.

| Emotional Need That Was Important to You | Mom | Dad |
|---|---|---|
| Being emotionally available to listen to me | | |
| Showing me physical affection with a kind touch | | |
| Saying "I love you" | | |
| Following through on a promise | | |
| Asking for my input | | |
| Helping me dream and envision my future | | |
| Celebrating my successes or accomplishments | | |
| Being dependable | | |
| Comforting me when I was hurting | | |
| Creating excitement | | |
| Showing pride in me | | |
| Respecting my opinions | | |
| Other: | | |
| Other: | | |
| Other: | | |

It's impossible to list every potential emotional need that goes unmet in childhood, so please use the spaces for other needs that aren't noted. Once you've completed this list, discuss it with your husband. Why is this helpful? Because he will then get a glimpse into why certain needs are particularly important when they aren't necessarily important to him. This can really help him trade places more effectively. And when you explore his most important personal emotional needs in the same way, you'll be doubly ready to help each other trade places. So once you've taken time to carefully consider these needs, be sure you take the time to discuss them with each other. Use examples from childhood to help your husband picture them.

# Your Time-Starved Marriage

## How to Stay Connected at the Speed of Life

*Drs. Les and Leslie Parrott*

This is not a book about being more productive — it's a book about being more connected as a couple. In *Your Time-Starved Marriage*, Drs. Les and Leslie Parrott show how you can create a more fulfilling relationship with time — and with each other.

The moments you miss together are gone forever. Irreplaceable. And yet, until now, there has not been a single book for couples on how to better manage and reclaim this priceless resource. The Parrotts show you how to take back the time you've been missing together — and maximize the moments you already have. *Your Time-Starved Marriage* shows you how to:

- relate to time in a new way as a couple
- understand the two lies every time-starved couple so easily believes
- slay the "busyness" giant that threatens your relationship
- integrate your time-style with a step-by-step approach that helps you make more time together
- stop the "time bandits" that steal your minutes
- maximize mealtime, money time, and leisure time
- reclaim all the free time you've been throwing away

Learn to manage your time together more than it manages you. Dramatically improve your ability to reclaim the moments you've been missing. *Your Time-Starved Marriage* gives you tools to feed your time-starved relationship, allowing you to maximize the moments you have together and enjoy them more.

Hardcover, Jacketed  978-0-310-24597-1

Also Available:

| | | |
|---|---|---|
| 978-0-310-81053-7 | Time Together | Hardcover, Jacketed |
| 978-0-310-26885-7 | Your Time-Starved Marriage | Audio CD, Unabridged |
| 978-0-310-27103-1 | Your Time-Starved Marriage Groupware DVD | DVD |
| 978-0-310-27155-0 | Your Time-Starved Marriage Workbook for Men | Softcover |
| 978-0-310-26729-4 | Your Time-Starved Marriage Workbook for Women | Softcover |

# Saving Your Marriage Before It Starts

## Seven Questions to Ask Before— and After— You Marry

*Drs. Les and Leslie Parrott*

A trusted marriage resource for engaged and newlywed couples is now expanded and updated.

With more than 500,000 copies in print, *Saving Your Marriage Before It Starts* has become the gold standard for helping today's engaged and newlywed couples build a solid foundation for lifelong love. Trusted relationship experts Drs. Les and Leslie Parrott offer seven time-tested questions to help couples debunk the myths of marriage, bridge the gender gap, fight a good fight, and join their spirits for a rock-solid marriage.

This expanded and updated edition of *Saving Your Marriage Before It Starts* has been honed by ten years of feedback, professional experience, research, and insight, making this tried-and-true resource better than ever. Specifically designed to meet the needs of today's couples, this book equips readers for a lifelong marriage before it even starts.

The men's and women's workbooks include self-tests and exercises sure to bring about personal insight and help you apply what you learn. The seven-session DVD features the Parrotts' lively presentation as well as real-life couples, making this a tool you can use "right out of the box." Two additional sessions for second marriages are also included. The unabridged audio CD is read by the authors.

The Curriculum Kit includes DVD with Leader's Guide, hardcover book, workbooks for men and women, and *Saving Your Second Marriage Before It Starts* workbooks for men and women. All components, except for DVD, are also sold separately.

Curriculum Kit  978-0-310-27180-2

Also Available:

| | | |
|---|---|---|
| 978-0-310-26210-7 | Saving Your Marriage Before It Starts | Audio CD, Unabridged |
| 978-0-310-26565-8 | Saving Your Marriage Before It Starts Workbook for Men | Softcover |
| 978-0-310-26564-1 | Saving Your Marriage Before It Starts Workbook for Women | Softcover |
| 978-0-310-27585-5 | Saving Your Second Marriage Before It Starts Workbook for Women | Softcover |
| 978-0-310-27584-8 | Saving Your Second Marriage Before It Starts Workbook for Men | Softcover |

# Love Talk

## Speak Each Other's Language Like You Never Have Before

*Drs. Les and Leslie Parrott*

A breakthrough discovery in communication for transforming love relationships.

Over and over, couples consistently name "improved communication" as the greatest need in their relationships. *Love Talk* — by acclaimed relationship experts Drs. Les and Leslie Parrott — is a deep yet simple plan full of new insights that will revolutionize communication in love relationships.

The first steps to improving this single most important factor in any marriage or love relationship are to identify your fear factors and determine your personal communication styles, and then learn how the two of you can best interact. In this no-nonsense book, "psychobabble" is translated into easy-to-understand language that clearly teaches you what you need to do — and not do — for speaking each other's language like you never have before.

*Love Talk* includes:

- The Love Talk Indicator, a free personalized online assessment (a $30.00 value) to help you determine your unique talk style
- The Secret to Emotional Connection
- Charts and sample conversations
- The most important conversation you'll ever have
- A short course on Communication 101
- Appendix on Practical Help for the "Silent Partner"

Two softcover "his and hers" workbooks are full of lively exercises and enlightening self-tests that help couples apply what they are learning about communication directly to their relationships.

Hardcover, Jacketed  978-0-310-24596-4

Also Available:

|  |  |  |
|---|---|---|
| 978-0-310-80381-2 | Just the Two of Us | Hardcover, Jacketed |
| 978-0-310-26214-5 | Love Talk | Audio CD, Abridged |
| 978-0-310-26467-5 | Love Talk Curriculum Kit | DVD |
| 978-0-310-81047-6 | Love Talk Starters | Mass Market |
| 978-0-310-26212-1 | Love Talk Workbook for Men | Softcover |
| 978-0-310-26213-8 | Love Talk Workbook for Women | Softcover |